I0459684

"Timothy Dodd almost cancelled his reservation at the Motel 8 of America, but he's glad he didn't. It's a good vantage point for people watching, and the sign is so bright you can see clear up into space. In *Galaxy Drip*, his latest poetry collection, Dodd's concerns haven't changed, but the setting has—contemporary America. He does seem more conflicted in these poems, but no less sure. Like any good poet, he equivocates (poetry is, in a sense, the art of equivocation). "Here is a truth," the poet says, "maybe." Dodd is no different in this regard. He wags a finger at our sad, crass consumerist twenty-first century America, but he also reaches out for it, because while he does not approve of it, he loves it (even if he says he doesn't) and elucidates with convincing specificity our uniquely American devolution. Whether it be a dying shopping mall, a smutty Circle-K, or a garish grocery store, Dodd sees something worth considering, even if he doesn't always think it's worth saving. "Whatever this is isn't progress," he says, "but it is fascinating." He offers no antidote to the sickness he sees because he isn't sure he wants it cured. What would the cure be, anyway? A pining for the past? A back-to-basics ethos? No, the past is not romanticized in *Galaxy Drip*. Nor is nature. Not even space…This book might be a sort of elegy to substance. Or, rather, the mourning of a substance that never was. Not here, at least."

—Steve Lambert, author of *The Shamble* and
The Patron Saint of Birds

"In *Galaxy Drip*, Timothy Dodd continues to explore the overwhelming realities of modern life as pop culture of the past and present fades in and out, then in again. Often with conflicting tones of sarcasm and sincere appreciation, he references the likes of Ambrose Bierce and Mark Twain next to Molly Hatchet, Madame Bovary to Kitty Pryde. Dodd shows advancement in his exploration of form with this collection, employing it to offer a grand flow of assorted images to the reader. Through the highways and hospitals, malls and shopping plazas, truck stops and corner stores, he reconciles the old with the new, writing about the people around him like an emotional journalist with empathetic eyes, offering cinematic depictions with uncanny depth and insight. This is a wonderful collection not to miss!"

—David Alec Knight, author of *Leper Mosh*
(Cajun Mutt Press)

Galaxy Drip

Poems by Timothy Dodd

LUCHADOR
PRESS

Luchador Press

Big Tuna, Texas

Copyright © Timothy Dodd, 2025

First Edition: 1 3 5 7 9 10 8 6 4 2

ISBN: 978-1-958182-96-3

LCCN: 2024948775

Cover image: Sanatorium Imereti: Tskaltubo, Republic of Georgia

    (Credit: Timothy Dodd)

Title page image: TNT Bunker, Mothman Zone: Point Pleasant, WV

    (Credit: Stephen R. Ramsey)

Author photo (back cover): Analie Siacor

Author photo (bio): Aiggee Patilan

All rights reserved. No part of this publication may be
reproduced or transmitted in any form or by any means,
electronic or mechanical, including photocopying,
recording or by info retrieval system, without prior
written permission from the author.

Acknowledgments

Acknowledgment to publications first publishing these poems:

"The Good & the Bad" and "Mark Twain & Me" in *Binnacle*,
"At the Kroger in Western Hills," "Today at Little Spike's BBQ,"
    and "Discarded" in *Perceptions: A Magazine of the Arts*,
"In Peacetime" in *I-70 Review*,
"Saturday Softly" and "The Great Convenience of the
    Automobile" in *Naugatuck River Review*,
"Athenaeum, New Year" in *Nova Literary Arts Magazine*,
"Pheromone Trails," "Midweek Luncheon," "Greyhound
    Stations," and "Storefronts" in *The Crucible*,
"Life and Death on Venice Street" in *Roanoke Review*,
"Boxers at Work" in *Suisun Valley Review*,
"Punxsutawney" in *The Loch Raven Review*,
"Triboluminescence" in *Rathalla Review*,
"To Taste" in *Sand Canyon Review*,
"Life in Fiction" in *Straylight*.
"Newsworthy" in *Silkworm*,
"Universal Commute" in *Stone Path Review*,
"Cholecystectomy" in *North Dakota Quarterly*,
"Post-industrial" in *Washington Square Review*,
"Cornstalk in Point Pleasant" in *GTK Journal*

Table of Contents

I. Commonplace Cryptids

II: Galaxy Drip

III. Confession of a Contemporary Depression

IV. The Last Krispy Kremes

The rain zigzagged across the show window in torrents and black gleaming umbrellas with frantic legs beneath were blown past. Market Street lamps were wet golden blobs dripping futile little puddles of light that made no difference to the black, wet night...

-Dance Night, Dawn Powell

"And the commercials would have sickened a goat raised on barbed wire and broken beer bottles."

-The Long Goodbye, Raymond Chandler

I

Commonplace Cryptids

Fuzzy Hieroglyphics

In the den's dry darkness
my dad nods off to sleep,
the Discovery Channel
now no match for a day
of installing cable TV.

The good Thomas & Abe
lie quietly together, sleeping
under Pops' old cushions,
hearing talk of a new day,
faux philosophy and theater.

I'm too young and hesitant
to make moves. For a roof
and three meals a day, I sit
and look around at little life's
spic and span expectation.

Mom soon calls down to stir:
"Food's ready, Ed!" He wakes
in stupor and drool with a lick
of his lips: "And bring up
a 2-liter Dr. Pepper, Doug."

Television flashes its temples
and Tutankhamen, a fatherly
grunt rises over the pharaohs
—snuffed out seconds later
by a White Cloud commercial.

The Good & the Bad

As I leave my apartment for the store,
stepping into bees of traffic, I think
how plows help grow my food, even
if supermarket tomatoes have no taste.

When my name is called to check blood
pressure and lift my knees for the doctor,
I think of our rise in life expectancy,
but then the rate of suicide in Finland.

When I turn off my night lamp to sleep
on my thousand-dollar bed, I recall
a village girl sleeping on the cold floor
with a brick as pillow; and my insomnia.

When I talk to my sister on the phone,
she tells me all her woes and bad luck.
I remember she's far away in Anchorage,
and how she stole my Halloween candy.

At the Kroger in Western Hills

we race through the parking lot in a downpour. Steve, my
    old high
school chum, grabs a cart to carry our little piles of selected
    sugars

and fats for our annual get-together. In the aisles, we point
    out our
mothers' favorite brands of baked beans and the barbecue
    Fritos

we shared for lunch when roaming Charleston High School's
    halls
like rabid rodents. Now, however, we can get gourmet if we
    want,

and the priciest cuts of meat. While looking at flavors of ice
    cream,
we run into Barry Schwartz in shorts, one of Steve's drinking
    pals.

While choosing cheese, I get introduced to Stan, therapist
    of Steve's
wife. Liz Stayon, who watches their Pekinese when they
    holiday

at the beach, pops up as we turn the corner to the bread
    section. Each
time I slink away, usual anti-social self. I trot over to check
    for new

varieties of juices instead, or contemplate tomatoes,
   wondering why
we left West Virginia. I ease over to the messy magazine
   section

to check if *Hit Parader* and *Circus* still get sold. In the
   checkout lane,
we load our items onto the counter, laughing at absurdities
   not worth

explaining. Steve whips out his Kroger card, and we watch
   as Sue
the cashier swipes our products through the price scanner.
   Steve pays

by credit card while I bag up, then we rush out and run
   through rain
again, carrying our yums to his used Mercedes. Twenty
   years ago,

we went grocery shopping with our moms, not each other.
   I glance
at Steve squinting in the deluge, his pressed slacks to my
   cargo pants,

sport coat to faded hoodie, bison leather zip boots to my
   ratty skate
shoes. I look at his contorted mouth and our aging features.
   Dear Janet

and Zenith: one gone, the other bedridden—we now look
   a lot like you.

In Peacetime

On another new Monday, the heads
of a city file off to work, carloads
settling soon into their cranky war—
the only way we Americans learn

new geography, some TV host said.
Our children will be simultaneously
schooled on simulacra, a little learning
optional. Some miles outside central
solutions, lost in the living room light,

George holds a postcard from Ukraine,
its face colored in Chagall: "Oh I didn't
know Gil's daughter could draw." Mary
sits in adjacent bathroom, half-hearing
her husband today in a different shade

of pink lipstick—spreading enough faith
to stave off cancer perhaps; commercial
colors they won't see in the new rubble,
old architecture starved by modern mob.

Entrées

The Chinese food here tastes different than it does in China, you know. So, too, the Indian, to a lesser extent. Then again, the food I prepare myself each day doesn't taste like me either—more like plastic and cardboard, preservatives. Am I that artificial?

Saturday Softly

At the midmorning playground, a young woman holds her
    child,
sets him down and watches as he waddles to the slicky
    slide. I am,

however, not welcome, and her stares want me to believe
    every
dying squawk from the birds is aimed at me. I have opened
    her

chest of fallout: grown men do not come to playgrounds
    to play.
And so it is best not to greet, I know—best not to smile,
    a further

risk of breakdown. What it means is: do not look at the
    hard curve
of the metal toy, the gleam of its smooth slide, or the
    rungs that let

you climb to higher ground for a moment of wild, joyful
    descent.
This is what got me here, I think—this is why I am always
    walking.

Go back to the diner for another cup of soup. Get lucky,
    get called
dear or honey, maybe even sweetie. Even childless codger
    will do.

Statehood

Sherry's sipping sherry,
        Dick's drinking whatever;

red Florida sky dazzling
        behind their new beach condo.

Wisps of tall marram grass
        drift at the edge of warm sand,

a retirement to Flagler floating
        with the same, just enthusiasm.

The Diamonds have called all
        coastal friends to celebrate, plus

a few strangers: it takes time
        for the sun to set, Dick thinks,

long enough to pour several
        of something. On ocean's edge,

where dunlins pick at tiny crab
        eggs, the captive engineer peers

out window, reminds himself this
        is paradise, maybe worth decades

of troubleshooting and squirmy
        anoles crawling across their walls.

Somehow Sherry doesn't seem
        to mind the lizards, and he forgets,

too, when rolling back to the toilet,
        unzipping linen shorts for another

porcelain fill up. Watching his final
        drips, he asks himself where all

his liquids go. Maybe onto the fins
        of whales to Mexico or India? Damn

geography, he thinks, heading back
        to patio for more chat on mussels, tans.

Athenaeum, New Year

On the library steps, face to glass
gives dark reflection, all the wars
and ancient Greeks locked inside
napping in a void of holiday cheer,
print all the more inconsequential
now to festive minds. Even streets
are calm, cars quieted in lit favors
of living room squawk and meaty
dinner tables. But from the outside
I peer in on postponed utility, old
ideas still new, forgotten features
once carved in marble. An earlier
search for immortality is unhidden
but unwanted. You cannot blame
the species living these occasions
of the moment any more than you
can blame me for hearing a silent
reverberation, wanting to be let in.

At the Shopping Center With
No Stores of Interest

There is insurance, nails, a pharmacy.
Chiropractor. Burgers & Chinese food.
Beer distributor. Two shoe stores.

Can you know a person, if you want,
by what they don't do and don't buy?

I never killed a lacewing, never went fishing,
never listened to Vivaldi as Molly Hatchet

wails. Walking by the video game store
I see a news reporter who stops me to ask,
"What excites you here?" Microphone

in my mouth, I say, I'm just looking
for someone who believes this is all trash,
all of it dying and we are on the periphery;

someone twiddling their thumbs in a secret
restroom, waiting for the coins to warp.

Obituaries

are like your dirty clothes
after a weekend camping trip;
only nothing's left to wash.

End Zone

I am getting nauseous on this job, although the fence
around school is high enough. I'm adequately socialized,

but the toilet paper gets thinner and more narrow each
year, inversely proportional. A utility man's head peeps

into the ceiling, mumbling to himself as I walk the halls.
Technology continues to improve, dropped on us again

and again like dead whales. Our leadership team—Talk
Talk was a great band—says students should be given

the chance to take more ownership in their education
and behavior. Our new nurse seems sickly despite just

replacing a deceased friend of mine. It is breast cancer
awareness week and the school is raising funds. Bring

your pennies Burger King slid back across the counter.
The school library is abandoned now, but lots of books

remain stuffed into shelves, lie out on tables. We have
not used it for anything related to books in years, only

for conferences and indefinite storage of broken printers,
computers, and copy machines. Well, there's a large filing

cabinet in middle of the bibliotheca, too, probably filled
with records someone once claimed were very important.

But don't worry: more standardized exams are on the way
and I am busy making sure I'm trained most appropriately.

If you take a close look, these tests might appear harmless,
if not pointless, but still I fear they may suck me in entirely,

absorb me into the absurdity of another ten-month school
year, this large brick building where I am lying in education.

Pheromone Trails

The little ants   here they come   there they go

   too many   to count.   They know

something   or smell it   dashing,

heading   for the sugar.   If there's a wall

barrier   dead end,   they will find   a way

to get around   continue course.

   There is a system to it   they've got down

I'm told—   I don't quite understand it

   despite a certain clarity   in their straight line

zipping   past   like a battalion of soldiers

sent   to fight for something   they might

believe in.   I wonder   when they will stop,

if they'll ever find a place of rest,   knowing

I cannot   only watch.   Somewhere

   in that chase   I jump in their lane,

join   the frantic race   down crowded highways.

Thoughts on Walking

In the old village, we could not walk far without a call, a
    greeting, or handshake.
In Erie, however, we all walk in solitaire, through the streets
    and supermarkets

with others we don't know. Loneliest places are commercial:
    crowded spots full
on commodified chat where oftentimes our most social act
    is a polite deferral, like

the brief pause we impatiently execute at a busy intersection
    when another driver
has the right of way. Otherwise, our walking feels oddly
    self-contained, adhering

to something like traffic regulations, navigating public
    spaces in our own airtight
minds: from Peel P50s to bulletproof limos. Walking into
    the woods is more rarity:

rivers and mountains no longer convenient enough. Walking
    neighborhoods gives
a different derivative: the earthy smell of wood burning,
    perhaps; artificial freshness

of laundry detergent; pineapple. Or how a policeman might
    direct me to an alternate
route—past the gas company whose dilapidated gate
    stretches around its perimeter:

an odd style to its curves and arches—art deco perhaps,
    with rusting around lovely
pale turquoise. How I might see a teenager in puffy
    Ponys; pudgy jacket, winter hat,

lumpish gait. I'll raise my hand to him, maybe to his
    trepidation. He'll give no reply.
I figure we're all trying to get some place, mostly
    somewhere called home, as secure

and convenient as possible. Maybe we're satisfied, at least
    partially, to believe in
a house in the middle of the block, an apartment building
    on the corner, a comfy pad

with odor-free carpet and modern appliances. Maybe it's
    my own tomfoolery, greed,
to imagine any and every place can be home. For no
    matter what I believe or wish,

I return to my own little post, too. The skittering motion
    on the ground aren't animals,
but plastic bags—although, walking home at dusk you
    can easily imagine all the same.

Today at Little Spike's Barbecue

All this cute consumerism means the menus get harder
    and harder
to follow. With niece at my side, I'm trying to sort out
    the sixteen

sauces swallowed up in colorful chalks and swirling fonts,
    decode
catchy platter nicknames in fine print. I'm trying to figure
    out how
their meal puzzles and prizes all fit together—which little
    section

holds the key: better head home to watch more commercials,
    Al;
pay more attention to Paramount Pictures and forget sun,
    soil, rain.

Life and Death on Venice Street

We've seen so many movies by now that when I see the
    hearse
from my bedroom window, pecking at the intersection,
    my brain

scrolls through a list of neighbors. Then I put my hand
    on heart
just to feel its rhythm, and take another sip of coffee.
    I spit it up

though when the doorbell rings, and I see the vehicle
    parked out
front. Has my wife died a second time? I put on a shirt,
    red, of all

colors, and open the door to a young woman attractively
    dressed
in black. She asks if anyone has died on the block, and
    then, when

I state I'm not one to say, asks me, in Hungarian, to
    accompany
her to the beach. "Jack won't go," she says. "Can you?"
    Except

for the coast of Nova Scotia, and Iceland, I haven't
    visited a beach
since I was a kid, ugly Myrtle, I think, remembering how
    I loathed

the scavenging seagulls, a roasted back, old chest hair and
    plastic-
looking, yellow toenails running loose, the vacationers
    lazily lined

up on the sand like a game show. But eyes in front of me
    shimmer
now, so I don't tell her this, just glance back at my childhood
    fresh-

faced—say sure with a run.

Midweek Luncheon

Looking up, workmates watch the sliding balls
          of the chockablock clock, fumbling
                    for a conversation piece in the atrium

before lunching at Strawberry Square's
          food court. Slices at Sbaro's...no, let's
                    swing by Beijing Sun, choose chop

sticks with Styrofoam cups, thin napkins,
          recycle gossip and office drama to the gristle
                    of beef with broccoli and hopes for a beerful

weekend. "Chad didn't even greet me
          this morning," the salty sauce spreads over
                    a tough chew and the hour slips away, only

enough left for a urinal leak and check
          of the hair, the dwindling of another noon-
                    time tune when even the unopened fortune

cookies get a quick flick, sail and settle
          into bag-lined trash cans, separated forever
                    from eternal jaunts back to high-rises

and a soft glide up elevators to worlds of paper
          clips and computers and meetings with slow
                    clocks and far too many words, wearing gray.

A Contemporary Novel Search
for Ambrose Bierce

From Golden State lives lift luxury antennae:
look look we believe in literary wonder, hero,

shopped across borders, perhaps quilting now
in Spanish. Recollect—unlike that full tank

of gasoline, a straight prose doesn't unlock all
the short-term secrets, doesn't capture earth's

possibilities. After two hundred miles, you still
need to stop for a cold beverage and grim relief

of the bladder. Plastic bags not worth the snack
inside can't contain culture clash, chile and lime;

meanwhile, do detail all your suffering please:
an unbearable heat, confiscation of the contact

lens, and an eyewitness to lies gone wrong, then
how injustice is such hurt here. Is your seatbelt

like an animal pelt—providing warmth? Does it
aid you in your afternoon yoga? Like the saints

in Paramount, we need our sleeping pills. Ninety
minutes and we call it all off for house slippers.

High-Rise on Elm Street

Slip into the downtown lobby of a megacity's summer
  buzz,
air conditioned ant farm. Slices of tree inside, Walker

grips his briefcase under a high ceiling, conscience
  hanging
down somewhere, surely, with a flag or two: a tap of his
  grey

shoes echo the help desk, passing a drooping alphabet's
  office
directory. Long lights suspended above keep me in an
  artificial

element uneasy on my ancestry. I pay electric bills here;
  clean
my teeth; fight pigheaded practices in pharmaceutical,
  landlord.

Standing on swirls of marble carved out of the ground,
  I await
one of four elevators to come and lift me, cozy box
  within a box,

button glow where I might get a stranger's tiny smile or
  a lot
of small talk framed by gazebos in trimmed urban park,
  floral

design, public art languishing in love like an on-the-job
    holiday
gift exchange: our sharing wrapped in sparkling, cold
    pretend.

II

Galaxy Drip

Veins

I am here at the next wedding, throwing handfuls
of ceremonial rice with Gia Carangi at the passing

cars, plumbers' vans, all driven by murderers. His
and her families mingle pride, the priest departed

after saying his few scripted, shallow words. Know
not bride nor groom, their mouths plugged deeply

into electrical sockets, we'll walk back to Abraham
Lincoln, peer into the education of dark weekend

windows and watch what birds still come our way,
dodging a sky of fashion and airplanes. When night

comes, we'll turn from the marriages tucked tightly
away. And speed down a night of Goodis' alleyways

to times goodbye, abandoned luncheonettes, sickly
explosions appearing on slick covers of magazines.

Quality Inn

Funny things mix inside the budget hotel
on Brigadier Ave: groggy respite shakes
hands with hair-clogged sinks, and family

vacations cuddle with company managers'
pleasurable liaisons. A convenient seven
blocks from the historical district, its clerk

sits and dwells on the past weekend,
missing little details such as thank you
and hello. Some people come a long way

for frozen waffles, plastic cups of orange
juice; some people couldn't find a better
deal. But with good gas mileage, maybe

the day is forgivable, maybe life is livable.
Maybe the coins clinking in the parking lot
soda machine are more than smooth metal

sliding through a void—perhaps neon lights
and the slight soothing of paid refreshment
can quench all of our dank, distant needs.

Capital Bowels

It's a capital city, not a Monstropolis—well, a state capital,
one said to have fallen on hard times; but this is twenty-first

century America—laden with concrete and metal and brick
and glass in replacement of trees. Still, a bird occasionally

flaps down to the belly of the transit(ory) center, curious
of vending machines beeping brightly like casino games,

their automated chambers awaiting smooth penetration
by Captain Coin in exchange for cold beverages and salty
chips, swallows of comfort and burp-defining independence.

Swanky rebelliousness hand in hand with luxurious injustice:
downright distasteful in the halls of hardware whose sockets

funnel more electricity than Catullus ever dreamed, a palace
now too commonplace for recognition by a motored citizenry

baking in the push-button glow energized by nickel, cadmium
sacked from other planets by little boys whose hands still dirty.

Mall Daze

Idling away in the drone of another empty wing,
        I'm stumped on a wooden bench carved

from some impressive tree felled in a country
        that might no longer exist. Grand smiles

hang from the wall, a touching welcome left three
        decades ago—somewhere, those faces

are not so photogenic now. Halls are hollowed
        and vacant—gone all my high school

friends, lovers, and the chatty sea of customers.
        But the faux marble tiles remain shiny

somehow, and the lights are still on, guzzling up
        electricity. The garbage bins in the corner,

once overflowing in deep sea plastic & Styrofoam,
        have set sail, may never need attending

again. And music keeps playing, mostly the same
        songs from those teenage years, so I sit

quietly watching the automated doors, waiting
        them to swing open, Daryl Hall to walk in.

Monumental Masonry Off Main Street

A shop selling tombstones:
chiseled markers of death in
granite stack gray selection.

Like the butcher who trims fat
from bone of the once living,
Frank Grim Monuments etches

the dates of the deceased, little
roses to make a moment smell
better. As with an automobile

that takes you around your city,
there are lots of choices: color,
design, and size—whatever it

takes to make you comfortable.
Outside, out of air-conditioned
offices, the grave markers lie

around like a room of sleeping
cats no longer flicking tails. I see
so many of them and start to think

the long stones of the dead must lie
under our feet everywhere we go,
burg or no burg, business or no

business—some independent
enterprise that started long before
Mr. Grim came to sell in town.

Life and Death in East Wheeling

Ambulance sirens blaze red at the end of the block,
the statue of St. Michael standing silently as traffic

flashes by in drizzle. The Salvation Army could not
save us of broken glass, busted schools: "For Youth

is Our Future" hangs on in lonely stone, its carved
impermanence cast to demolition queue. But clean

windows sparkle at Channel 13 News, kissing us
with "For Hire" signs, cameras rolling for our TV

screen sieves. In thick air float strange opportunities,
and I think a moment of all the empty little jobs we do.

.

Down Below

From the Super 8 rooftop I can
count the boxes of lab work sitting
outside the pediatrician's door:
blood, urine, stool—gods all
with twelve-chapter novels to sell.
The Red and the Black sandwiches
his and her brownish-yellow liquid,
diamonds for ant-boys in remote-
controlled Matchbox cars that circle
but never prod in their crumb-carry
to a never-to-be-seen queen who,
maybe, can state which characters
have cancer or who developed kidney
stones amidst the little bags of potato
chips swirling now as sidewalk flowers,
Wendy's red pigtails beginning to blur.

Greyhound Stations

are where our real elopement begins, where an American
divorces her car for true love, even though less than one

percent of all U.S. citizens have inhaled the wingdripped
crusty pigeon bridge of our nation's mighty bus terminals;

that's about the same number answering in the affirmative
to a national poll asking if bus companies named after dog

breeds are a good idea: dachshund to Dalmatian, whichever
cuddles nicely in a dirty corner when your trip gets delayed.

Central Location

There's a small regional airport near
my home, although I've never seen it.
Still, jets fly right over my apartment.
I guess someone's up there sipping
red wine through impractical clouds.

And the boulevard is one block away
from me. All day the cars race past—
people going to New Jersey, downtown,
or other places. The hospital is right on
the other side. I had an operation there,

walked home after discharge. I wonder
still where the blood came from. Three
transfusions, that is. Blood banks down
the boulevard, sure. Before that? Bloke
from Albuquerque, Aberdeen? A girl

from Zanzibar? So many places I have
never been—most places. Many places
I don't know, can't spell. For example,
Ojibwe. Places maybe rippling through
my veins now in fact. Like a river after

spring rains. By the way, the river is also
six blocks past the boulevard. It's called
the Delaware, but no one travels by boat
anymore. If you walk to it, however, you
will pass by a very large prison still in use.

Dead/Lines

I'm racing through rowdy avenues
to gravestones standing history:

the presidential and mad, mothers
and loves of poet, traitor, defender;

all laid to casket, surrounded by
the mess of modern roads, traffic.

Truth is, I'd never crossed the border
to Richmond, and with only six hours

passing through, I've mapped out
my destinations: Oakwood, Shockoe

Hill, and Hollywood. Our distances
and opening hours matter now: since

my morning train arrived, I've scorched
the pavement rambling down sidewalks

and streets, jaywalking, cutting across
city squares and parking lots at a torrid

pace. In these city moments, sounds all
run together, bury better judgments until

I almost forget: our tear toward tombs
only hastens an interview with the dead.

Nail City

In the morning I step off the Heritage Trail, loitering
along landscapes where concrete gets chewed. Time
is trimming our pilgrim steps, screws, but hardware
stores hang on and vintage names still creep in crack
across dusty thresholds, lingering a little longer than
even commerce sanctions. There is the Tuberculosis
Ass., Odd Fellows Building, & West Virginia Snakes
Club. This is Wih-ling, Weeling, don't forget—place
of the skull. Our ephemeral victory gaggled decades
skinning their clairvoyance, yet a quiet canoe keeps
adrift on the Ohio, ready to reclaim hunting grounds.
Modern memory is short-lived, but I read historical
placards nonetheless. Scarred and ignored, cursed in
graffiti, I ponder the place—our past a blurred dream.

Advancement and Atrophy

On Roosevelt Boulevard, near the beer distributor
which used to be Empire Rock Club where bands
like Cinderella, Britny Fox, and Tangiers started
careers in the early days of hair metal, a Checkers
drive-through kiosk rots at the corner of Rhawn.
Now semi-fenced, boarded up, and graffitied, drug
needles, potato chip bags, and an old mattress litter
the ground near its busted window. Only its retro
logo and sign lifting up toward highway lights holds
its original condition. One morning at dawn I walk
by, hundreds of cars and trucks zipping past every
minute. In the buzz I think how grease has stopped
sizzling. No more milkshake slurps through straws,
and the teased hair and makeup at the end of guitar
melodies, shrieks, and drum rolls are gone. Groans
of cattle getting dragged into abattoirs in Delaware
have quieted. Except for traffic frying these roads,
the only signature remaining is the quietest: pink
swirls, bands, washes, and blazes of eternal sunrise,
coloring us above like diluted streaks of blood left
below one day by our easy addiction to automobiles.

Screenshots

We see blood on the snow, red,
not in the stew where bananas
traveled from Nicaragua, injected
with a coat of makeup to hide her
skin defects from a creaky priest,
his hard wand waving soft words
about eternity at the wedding,
celibate and freezing great lives
outside our windows, not in beds
from where we turn the channel
to visit Paris and birds of paradise
in permanent zoo like us, under
the ground where ecosystems live
never found and bodies of the dead
hear the wind better than we do.

Punxsutawney

crawls with groundhogs: both fat
and skinny ones; some stand smiling,
others sit expressionless. Almost all
were never real. Some are dressed
in Scottish kilts, with bagpipes to blow.
Some wear top hats while others carry
American flags or play banjos. Some
grace town murals, others are souvenirs
car-carried far away. See, here in Punxsy,
we make national headlines once a year
for Groundhog's Day...cause of Phil
...the critter who predicts winter's end
when emerging from his hole. Our lone
non-groundhog sculpture, wood carved,
is a moccasin-wearing native standing
in front of the police station. No surprise
he's got a peace pipe, spear, and quiver
slung over his back as well. Nameless,
of unidentified tribe, a sign to his left
reads: "Punxsutawney - Name of Indian
Origin—Founded 1818." That's law
and order now, but I wonder if it's better
just to sculpt another groundhog: Phil
and his family haven't yet been railroaded
or forgotten. And they're not all that bad
in the grand scheme of things really, just
tubby, little creatures like me. Harmless.
So I say to myself: be thankful we're not
the town of squid or sole. Or scat. Thank
great God and country we're not the town
of Mick Jagger, proctology, or my ex-wife.

III

Confession of a
Contemporary Depression

The Short Story

As the water heats up for afternoon tea,
Chekhov is laid out on the chair—a ratty,
mildewy hardback copy from the Butler
library wrapped in a faded see-through
cover. *Later Stories*, it's called, with tales
of love and prostitution and nervousness,
marriage; mostly depression roaming on
through social situations and samovars,
expectation and disappointment, failures

in contentedness. Another ancient flaring
of the age-old plot: steam rising and her
leaving. Boris glaring at the temperature
surge, rumbling in his apartment toward
an irreconcilable boiling point, the final
scene that will surely end with a—*click*—
the electric kettle flips off   —*bang*—
and gunshots bleed to silence: two dead,
sprinkles of sugar falling between pages.

Would They Shower in the Dark?

Elevators, up and down
they jog, with a cart
full of rainy seasons; high-
rise smiles hiding in blue
uniforms. In thick sauce
stones sleep in an exhaust
pipe, all the burn belched
out in tummy trimming
workouts. Where is she?
Eye, where is the Ferry?
Late again, trapped in bed
traffic, the morning alarm
a downpour on drowning.

Triboluminescence

In those celestial explosions, one might
think   the night itself is tired,
weary of looking down   on men,
women   at their tables
spitting words   their oil
burned and dried saying he cuts
fingers every Wednesday evening,
          practically steals elegant wines
—at good prices. Meat first,
scraped away   under invented
lights. Expectations more canned
than raw
                    only starting the twinkle
is that wintergreen Lifesaver
                    crunched in his jaw
      not a secondhand comet
once ridiculed behind glass.   We are
broken   chemical bonds
flickering for a change   praying
to unite once more   create
new stars   in a dying galaxy.

To Taste

From a great confusion,
our coincaused continental
drift, she picked a brick
not a blackberry, shoved
it sideways in her mouth,
said it sweetness. Years later
she vomited in forgotten field
filled with tall, tick-riddled
timothy where her child buried
himself with plastic and twine,
unsure why a simple fruit
the size of a quarter, its smell
now manufactured in a bottle,
didn't digest after a century
of waste. We must lick air
at net-cost, they told her
by cellular—the tar-tamed,
escape-a-lunged, bodied in
factories sunk in slimepit.
But bushes, where? Thickets,
countryside walks, fruits
fulfilled? Will they fall again
to birds emptying juices in
sweet song or only stiff-railed
platforms piling up pills?

The Great Convenience of the Automobile

Each early morning, we millions believe: worker
ants for our colonies. Not reaching for Seminole
forests, the edge of Ontario, or the lips of El Paso.

Red light.

And what does she think, dental hygienist, sipping
on her brew. She parks on Pistol Street, to pick on
teeth, then jumps back in behind a sunset wheel.

Stop sign.

On to Cosco for frozen shrimp bucketed off western
Thailand's coast. And a New Zealand zinfandel. But
only after pulling in to the Wells Fargo ATM. Did I

Toll booth.

forget Peggy's Pets for the toenail clipping? No, no,
that's Saturday when Tush is on board. Today, Evan's
daycare, then Wow Cow How for a pint of fudge ripple

Parking lot.

and a gallon of organic milk. Don't forget the Lord
& Taylor blouse to return and...Hi Mary Lou mother-in-
law, I can't talk right now—call you back—the shrimp

Stuck in traffic.

is thawing, ice cream is melting, Tush is barking. I
mean Evan's crying...I need to reach Rite Aid before
the pharmacy closes...I'm out of Vanatrip...drop off

Road work.

the electricity bill at the post office...pick up baby
formula at GNC...and Exxon, Exxon, Exxon...only
a little gas left in the tank...almost empty...almost asleep.

Head-on collision.

Silent Song

Aphids swarm night cosmos at the window,
its cracks and glass our buzzing viewpoint.

Forgotten factories wilt slowly, shadowing an
unknown, crumbling among our daylighting.

Beetlecrawl over the marble tiles us silently,
our efforts darkened gateways to deep earth.

There's a disgust to all of our happiness—
a strained swallow to the pride of existence.

Static Inn

We sit, ready to remains—the hotel bottling
our loneliness, capped to carry and prepared

to pour into love's see-through glass, ice down
a distant hallway. Hopper-hung, we are empty-

roomed, strangers to the art dressing our walls.
Simulating satisfaction by turning on switches

and gadgets, our dressers have neither emperor
nor clothes, our window a view onto nobody's
future with a bed in the corner, comforter used.

There might still be voices down in the foyer:
great illusion that our chat is connection rather

than an ad away from television. Disguised as
the living, we listen, eavesdrop on long guests

checking out in a lobby whose piano is lost,
melodies of a reservation we'd like to cancel.

Life in Fiction

I am molded and plied,
cemented by my author
from his hardened chair

in a small downtown Chicago
college. I am office inked
to lie inside a soulless stack

of bleached papers, poetic
as glue-trapped mice. I am
wooden performance grunt,

a stranger's callous need, cut
up protagonist for study
in his award-winning dream,

a bookmarked villain
living a panel's pomp,
longing for my own name.

Death of My Lover

Tripping through Erie traffic, I
pass the crematorium, her smells

still on me: peach skin lotion, Tide,
bodily fluids. Marriage certificates

can burn, too, pastor, father, squid,
—squat & shoot without cornering

me. I have searched for wild fruits
having no English names, but now,

on the sidewalk, I inhale engine
exhaust, the corpse of incinerating

vehicles that drone past, tense, like
contemporary prayers to conquer

death. Anna also rides in a casket
of cars, going far away, but it's her

life I still smell, not her end, dying
as she searches alleys for new love.

Love Like a Comet

I might not be
                    the one
            to cross your "t"
            and dot your "I"
                    cross "t" again …
                    Or anyone's.

I might be   rather
            a bedbug
            a tick
            or pubic lice … crabs
                    and consistently so.

But I never asked
            for Madame Bovary,
            Kitty Pryde.
I never wanted
            Angela Joline.

I am not
            their marriage
            certificates
            or Breeders Cup
                    you know what I mean.

Modern physics has left
            me in quarks and tears
            a theory of relativity

And creative writing teaches
        show don't tell
        and, please, no clichés.

Mangos, thyme, and coconuts
        taught me
        sweetness, yes, bloom
        to savor even
        when not consuming.

But they don't walk
        into nightclubs
        cinemas
        dance parties
        where Russian
        Roulette increases
        your chances,
        and Pushkin's old queen
        has a sweet, sensitive nose.

They don't tell me to pump
        up my pecs,
        get a gourmet
        haircut, whip out
        fashion and credit
                cards.

So love, to me, is a night blur.
Love is in outer space,
        is outer space
        forgetting the name
        of that comet flying past

in a whirr, with a tail
every seventy-five years
                    or so.

Mark Twain & Me

On that wide Mississippi
cutting through new world,

something red floats by—
a plastic container of sorts.

I watch it drift, wondering
what's inside, what value

could be mine should I reach
out, pull it in, open to find

gems, games, gold: see, hold,
cast into my pockets to hide

from others sharing bone. Us,
we go: routed in floating desire,

meaning a mystery locked
in passing vessels, never ours.

Nomads

On a cold December walk from the Rite Aid,
floating past Al's corner diner, gym, traffic

—squat thrusts, a meatball grinder, speeding,
and I get this feeling that I'm really ready to go

to *that* netherworld: no fighting it, no savage
droop or despair. Then I look at a little house

on the block: compact, immobile, still; locked
in, all its life lived in this gravid town. On my

side of the street, bunches of starlings piddle
and peck in an old age home's yard, too early

to get back to parasite-infested dens. Scrubby
little transplants like me, some in breadmouth,

we, benefiting from human's cut, clip, and trim.
In swarm, they are city, the boisterous driving

of an old collective will over the green; loudest
might one day be first to go, I think, leaving

this land as silent bell. Behind wires and tools,
nothing much is found after removing the case;

instead, mix my finger with their beaks, donkey
tail, vanadium. We'll all be on time at the waltz,

dancing in forgotten medicine and carrying tiny
canisters of lighter fluid, once city day is done.

Boxers at Work

Only the laundry room
knows his lime green
shorts, for in the office
they hide under dark
grey suits as he phones
and files, traffic sliding
outside the window.
Courting commerce,
cash pins him down
with a count, but at lunch
he manages to sneak out
for allergy medication
and a peak in Dillard's:
a nod to overshadowed
tastes, feelings cloaked
day to day by acceptable
tones, and secrets worn
under very fine clothes.

IV

The Last Krispy Kremes

Newsworthy

With this paper cut and cup
       of blood for my black
       pudding, I see finger
       pointing, sensational-
       ism and a bite of self-
       importance. Between

bargains and baggy pronouns,
       bipolar and political
       polls, I've neatly noted
       Maybelline isn't make-be-

lieve. But between hit-and-run
       coverage, I fail to find
       an update on sloth (maned)
       or bat (gray). I missed

news that said people run in fear,
       don't like such animals
       much; instead, like school-
       boys, spitting and tossing
       rocks at roost and perch.

I only learned bats spread rabies,
       and sloths are dirty. But
       what about mammalian
       marvels called echolocation
       or slow metabolism? What
       about an annihilation sliding

through our veins, vampired
on e-waste and aluminum

alloy? Sitting in my Toyota at the red
light, pecking at my new Galaxy
(Samsung), some other amazing
facts got left out of my news:
the sounds made by our Christmas
Island pipistrelle, now extinct,
and that the healthiest polar bears
are stuffed and smiling on satin sheets.

Virus Rx

The pharmacy is dark inside,
of lights no one needed. All
of us are healed by a string
that prances in cold weather.
There is a sale on medication,
a satisfaction in the symptom,
but don't speak of emptiness
inside when the pills get locked
away and no one wants to wait
on the sun for another old refill.

Well of the World

In the parking lot the stray canine
paws at the garbage can until it tips,

scouring for cafe waste. I wonder
from my seat on the bus, what it is

I sniff once the meat is paid for
and I've got a soft bed in sunlight.

Trash is now scattered at the entrance
even of my meals. Yet I still eat

chopped, bloodied, stolen, endangered,
as long as it's tender, with garlic, tasty,

consuming until the stomach begins
to balloon, its shape drawn by ghosts

in the dark while I sleep with thoughts
less than a dream: licking up the spoils,

believing what falls out is mine, all mine.

Universal Commute

Explosion collapses the core, bursting
frowns and scowls into purple fog-
cloud matter of burning gas, spinning
exhaust through the black tar void to be
"on-time." Now horns bleed as collision
heats: speeding steel, scars, and sizzle.

A crust forms as the surface cools, rivers
blooming from the cracks and graves
of stars. From twisted highway wreckage
we don't see new planets form, brilliance
in death teaching a lost kind of patience.

Cholecystectomy

These bruises from gallbladder removal
are some of my favorite colors: purples
and pinks that fondly recall Lake Kariba
sunsets, the hippos' eyes watching where
I might move next. I'm no hippo myself,

still thin and mobile and rarely, if ever,
aggressive. I'm no Tonga either, displaced
by the dam. So much that we do today,
accomplishments I suppose, is marvelous,
shrewd, yet somehow invasive all the same:

your uplifting dinner is another creature's
tragedy, demise. Some days we eat sweetly,
until one morning the hard pain in our gut
is too much to continue, and so we're cut
open to an increasingly common surgery,

the procedure of which, the more I think
about it, tells me I still cannot fathom much
of anything at all. Atop everything, if you
ask me, lies irony: a medicine with its own
side effects perhaps, certainly a different

route to the cure. Maybe what goes around
comes around, I'm not sure: we seem to have
dismissed that philosophy lately, but I for one
smiled in confidence when I asked the surgeon
where he was from and Baghdad was his reply.

Afterimage

What happens after our revolution—
the industrial one—when all the fuel
goes away, when we cannot pack up
on weekends for a getaway or reach
the doctor by telephone, when we no
longer can purchase throat lozenges
or even reach the store, when our food
is no longer delivered. We'll see only
birds in the sky and water of the river,
coolness from rain and jokes we can
make ourselves. I imagine many will
die, more animals will live, and plants
will grow. There will be fewer deals
to make and a great sadness of clocks
waiting to be invented. We may learn
the language of cows again: although
their sounds remain the same, what
changes are the ears to listen. We may
learn of blessing and curse; we might
speak to mud, adjust to light, distance,
age, and size; we might learn, in fact,
that life still bears in ancient children.

Without a Car

the moon scanned at the corner, fits of Amish
          on a captive engine; freedom a ghostly chance,

or thundering platitude at the stoplight, what could
          roll by in little to cover, reveal. See green

in the ocean, blue on forest floor, a violet in bruise
          and sky, loud temperature in the motor

locked out for new species of bird. Drive us out, on
          to despair, catching four wheels to Oslo's

Kierkegaard maybe, all the glamour of a continent
          in another loud Ford commercial:

the drag in someone's continence, payment deferred
          for the belief that God rolls down our highway

forever.

Post-industrial

these crumbling buildings lose
                              their language;
so, too, our lives in the whip
                              of vehicle mob
buzzing by as if to a utopian
                              space colony,
our great chase to indebtedness
                              empty vessels:
we tie on the more practical shoe,
                              limping for logo,
the supernal lost in us, measuring
                              distance instead
with plans of driving the gap to zero
                              all in one tongue;
we've stopped looking at the craft
                              of old buildings:
cut them straight now, grind
                              without noticing
how they once bent windy days
                              like wildflowers.

Usurpers

Our cocky taxidermy now claws vacant forests,
chameleon eyes still spinning their rusty knives
that sliced open the bulge of generations. More

for us remains, we're cocksure, even after a last
creature has fallen. Otherwise, time for the exotic,
crawling only on tribal continents like tiny bogus

spirits of the ancient dead. The gecko lost might
find a little luck limping to an abandoned veranda
—or surely some swamp-slimed amphibian can

hold a rattling chain against extinction. Echoes
of leopard walk, in the meantime, are styled scams;
fossilized footprints a form of primitivism staffed

as a fortress of cannibalism. Animal possession
has consumed us: wild the prosperity; all claims
against it a silent shriek dried up to domination.

Nice Evening (The New Environmentalism)

It's refreshing when the chef of Pacchia is in
your dining room, enjoying your meaty lasagna.
In fact, he likes it so much he finishes off a healthy portion
in four great bites, including the tinfoil
and even the fork itself. Then the plump little fellow
(from Toledo) tosses back the Chardonnay from Bulgaria,
just gulps it down, glass and all. Dessert isn't yet served,
so he takes to the napkin, with its little grease stains
shaped like livers, then the tablecloth, sucks that
down his windpipe too. When I return with Lady
Fingers, he's eaten the table itself, my photographs
from the Grand Canyon, Amy Hempel books,
two moths hovering around the light, a box of clothes
I had packed for Goodwill. "I'm starving," he says.
Before long the walls themselves are resting inside
his stomach, the floor, the ceiling, even the air
in the room is swallowed, and we're left standing
in a void that only a physicist could explain.

But I don't mind. Now I won't need to do dishes tonight
or inhale cold lasagna remnants. I won't have to take the trash
out on Friday, won't block the sidewalk for the two people
who walk around Alexandria instead of drive—they mostly
wear Duke t-shirts and look into clothing shop windows.
Instead I can watch the nuthatches poke up and down
the pines in the park outside my bedroom,
their queer noses upturned, otherwise a bit like the chef's.
And the landfill, somewhere far across the Potomac,
will get a brief reprieve, a quick moment to take a deep breath
until the next pile of meaty look-alikes is dropped on its chest.

From Inside Our Hearths

The crows comb through yogurt containers stuck
    between ribs,
tin foiled pick of our murder, closing in on the weapons
    tossed

out in Glad bags, prodding and stabbing the excess of
    midweek
feasting under secured lids. Father's fury shoots saliva
    at sprayed

Windex. Shoo them. Spray them. Scream them. Shoot,
    wings
flapping beneath terrycloth robes. But still they return—
    return

wearing Emily's red panties, dangling from cracked beak,
    dripping
with fat juice. At night, the congregation gathers, looking
    down

at sinners. But morning brings the dumping, locked into
    curbside
services, pecking our grandchildren photogenic, carrying
    off flowers

arranged for Grandma's viewing, her limp. They sort
    through our
television hearts, lifting bloodied and boogered Kleenex
    from new

floral handbags: beaks climbing stairs to ancestral quilts,
    to drink of
our toilets. Nothing hauled away. They return: salvaging
    moldy

hymnals of a risen Christ; picking at artificial nails
    wrapped in wet
wipes; saving cosmopolitan weekends from one-way
    streets. Collecting

plastic faith, our faith in plastic, misgivings, misguidance,
    in greedy
reflection, the light tackling silver fillings while flossing
    our smiles.

Watch them rummage with delusions of gold eye. Biting
    us in pyrite,
winging to delicate trees we don't see in microscope,
    fracking all

our throats. Reincarnated feasts, fixtures of our caw,
    blood earth,
mountain refrain. Nothing is burned but a return, to us,
    in mirror.

Storefronts

In all our cities, dead eyes hang
behind windows, weaving cotton
stares in blindness. Lost, one fish
at a time, they ask the netted how
to kick off designer shoes—reed
baskets empty. Bees don't buzz
where Mrs. Bonito buys her clover-
scented candles, flowers of all kinds
clipped for quarters. Smell them,
model, smell the raffia skirts burn
in perfume, in line, checking-out
all we cannot purchase now that
ancient graves are marketed mall.

Warmed Winter

It's middle of February now and not
even cold. We, the vast majority, are
pleased: fewer shivers and shakes. We
can go around now with less stress,
physically speaking: quicker to heat
the Mazda in the morning for example.
Like the day our boss is out of office
we can shed what isn't wanted, we can
go around in less winter wear: scarves,
gloves, thick coats, whatever covers
our ears. Our recreation, too, avoids
setback: it's cozy enough to go with Sy
for rosemary braised lamb shanks over
saffron rice, mint tea. No snow shovel
either, and no icy roads to endanger
our babies in baskets. Even the flu bug,
friend of the frigid, leaves us alone,
our lives all the brighter. Sure, it's still
saintly to saunter down to the Sunshine
State for a week's jewel in January, but
there's no need to return to Jack Frost
or a turn on of fiery furnace. Maybe we
won't appreciate the breaking of spring-
time so much now, that might potentially
be a drawback—but who really cares?

Discarded

Chicken bones scattered on the subway floor:
even if you don't believe in reading coffee

grinds, palms, or anything of the sort, you may
wonder what it all means: are we full or empty,

satisfied or in despair? Every seat is occupied,
many with bags of holiday merchandise refusing

owners' laps: games and purses and toys and sex
toys and fan gear and balls and pillows, perfumes

to smell and comfy shoes and candy-striped bed
sheets. Doors close behind me and I grip the pole,

hold on. These are the cheap seats now, not for
Rolling Stones or Yankees or even circus acts.

So could we take these skeletal remains, grab
our duct tape, hot glue guns, superglue, sticky

putty, magnetic tape strips, wax, sugru, and put
bones back together again? Acquire dirty grey

feathers at arts and craft stores, Vacation Bible
School, or online? Use more adhesive, add glass

eyes, form the beak from eggshells? Could we
then breathe the breath of life into this animal?

Let it walk again, walk the subway, out the doors,
into our cities, battle-tested, ready for our coffee

containers, job interviews, frozen foods dropped
into a vat of oil, miles seen through windshields,

and half our holiday gifts now stuffed into closet.
End of the line, out of time, nothing comes alive,

but another bone gets tossed on the floor, rolls just
near my shoe, made from leather, cow, not chicken

nor bone. Humans stand up when the subway stops,
gather their overblown, overgrown, mammoth bags,

walk through the steel doors, perhaps to a Popeyes,
a lingerie store, or a rodeo. To their heated homes.

Fly Agaric

Bright red mushrooms
splatter the forgotten
football field like drops
of blood. She will come
to pick me up, cheap ride
to the unknown, leaving
my little boring grasslands
barren of crops, where
enemies once chatted,
mountain lions kissed.

Cornstalk in Point Pleasant

Cheek to cheek, or mouth to neck,
we procreate, like a train wreck
of wails and whines. And we cherish
our children's wine, never far from the track.
We blanket them in dreams of want,
the cheap bliss of more gifts, of fancy
feathers to forget the cheat.

Let us grow strong, for strong is beautiful.
Let us put diamonds on fingers, in our ears,
under our holes of coal and gases.
Let us expand, claim all the hunting grounds,
claim that destiny draws the lines, to say mine,
to say legal, to say right is right. By birth
and by God, the rest doesn't matter. David deserves
not a deer's hoof, but a highway to hound
gold and hump a hundred high heels.

> Under the monument lies our chief, flattened
> for the faded afternoons of vacant stares
> that pass through town
> like measly clouds lost in a drought,
> on their way to where the stars are buried.
>
> "Hi ho." Were they not acquitted of murder?
> "Hi ke ho wa se li si mi mo?"

For *our* cheeks are pockmarked
not by love or lust, but by hammer
blows, sugared teeth and gasoline.
There is rarely a rise anymore
from these alcohol-damaged gullies:
neither language, nor pride,
nor our pant-plagued peckers.

Only 200 of us are left, aged and tired:
tired of hearing their bodies press
together in couponed check-out lanes,
tired of their phrase "making love,"
tired of their thrusting of spears into loins,
of smacks and rubs and groans
that never sounded as lovely
as all our extinct languages,
now almost glad to be dead.

Sliding Rock Rest Stop

The few open parking spots are marked handicap.
18-wheelers on I-76 whirr behind me in the distance.
People are pouring out with Popeye's and Burger King
    boxes, Starbucks coffees.
People seem wider than they were last year here.
The huge garbage bins are full of plastic
        and an iPad-plugged, jean-clad youth throws
                in more.

In the Kwik-Mart, a woman proclaims that Twix are
    getting tinier all the time.
There are more than 60 varieties of cigarettes.
Mountain Dew now comes in orange and purple and
    berry.

The urinal I draw is a bit backed up with the previous
    guy's liquid and a pink puck to piss on.
They are out of paper towels, but there are several
    wadded on the floor.

This is where we rest. This is where we get out and
    stretch our legs.
This is where we eat. And drink. And urinate.
    And defecate.
This is our cycle.

How much longer until we reach our destination?

Timothy Dodd is from Mink Shoals, WV in the heart of the Appalachian Mountains. He is the author of short story collections *Fissures, and Other Stories* (Bottom Dog Press), *Small Town Mastodons* (Cowboy Jamboree Press, forthcoming), *Men in Midnight Bloom* (Cowboy Jamboree Press), and *Mortality Birds* (Southernmost Press, with Steve Lambert), as well as poetry collections *Orbits 52* (Broadstone Books, forthcoming), *Modern Ancient* (High Window Press) and *Vital Decay* (Cajun Mutt Press). His stories have appeared in *Yemassee, Broad River Review, Anthology of Appalachian Writers*; his poetry in *Roanoke Review, Crannog, The Literary Review, Crab Creek Review,* and elsewhere.

Also a visual artist, Tim primarily exhibits his work in the Philippines. This includes his solo exhibition *Come Here, Nervousness* at Manila's Art Underground, as well as *Secondhand Smoke* (with Gerecho Iniel Cruz) at Mono8 Gallery. His expressionistic oil paintings can also be sampled on both Instagram timothybdoddartwork and timothy doddart.crevado.com. Tim completed his B.A. in comparative religion at Wesleyan University in Middletown, CT, and his MFA in the bilingual creative writing program at the University of Texas El Paso. He is an avid traveler and has spent extensive time in such places as Zimbabwe, Chile, Ethiopia, and the Republic of Georgia. Visit him at timothybdodd.wordpress.com.

This project was made possible, in part, by generous support from the Osage Arts Community.

Osage Arts Community provides temporary time, space and support for the creation of new artistic works in a retreat format, serving creative people of all kinds — visual artists, composers, poets, fiction and nonfiction writers. Located on a 152-acre farm in an isolated rural mountainside setting in Central Missouri and bordered by ¾ of a mile of the Gasconade River, OAC provides residencies to those working alone, as well as welcoming collaborative teams, offering living space and workspace in a country environment to emerging and mid-career artists. For more information, visit us at www.osageac.org

Osage Arts Community

www.ingramcontent.com/pod-product-compliance
Lightning Source LLC
Chambersburg PA
CBHW030459130626
46549CB00007B/2792